# LIFE AT EXTREMES
# UNDERGROUND

## Josy Bloggs

W

First published in Great Britain in 2023
by Hodder and Stoughton

Copyright © Hodder and Stoughton 2023

Editors: Julia Bird; Julia Adams
Design: Peter Clayman
Illustrations: Josy Bloggs

HB ISBN 978 1 4451 8384 8
PB ISBN 978 1 4451 8385 5

MIX
Paper from
responsible sources
FSC® C104740
FSC
www.fsc.org

10 9 8 7 6 5 4 3 2 1

Franklin Watts, an imprint of
Hachette Children's Group
Part of Hodder and Stoughton
Carmelite House
50 Victoria Embankment
London EC4Y 0DZ

An Hachette UK Company
www.hachette.co.uk
www.hachettechildrens.co.uk

Printed and bound in Dubai

The website addresses (URLs) included in this book were
valid at the time of going to press. However, it is possible that
contents or addresses may have changed since the publication
of this book. No responsibility for any such changes can be
accepted by either the author or the Publisher.

# CONTENTS

INSIDE EARTH ............ 4

TECTONIC PLATES ............ 6

ALWAYS CHANGING ............ 8

UNDER OUR FEET ............ 10

UNDERGROUND CAVES ............ 12

CAVE DWELLERS ............ 14

BURROWS ............ 16

LIFE BELOW GROUND ............ 18

SAFE HIDEAWAYS ............ 20

HIDDEN NETWORKS ............ 22

UNDERGROUND RICHES ............ 24

DIGGING UP THE PAST ............ 26

THE FUTURE ............ 28

GLOSSARY ............ 30

DIG DEEPER ............ 31

INDEX ............ 32

# INSIDE EARTH

Earth is covered by land masses and huge oceans that stretch across two-thirds of its surface. Both land and water are a rich habitat for living things, but below Earth's surface is a completely different environment that has so far been little explored.

## Earth's layers

Inside, Earth is made up of layers of extremely hot rock and metal. Nuclear reactions in the centre of the planet (the core) radiate heat to the outer layers. We catch a glimpse of this fiery heat when magma travels up from inside Earth as part of a volcanic eruption.

## Crust

The crust is the outermost and thinnest layer. It is made up of rock. Under the oceans, the crust is thinner and mostly consists of basalt. Under land, the crust is thicker and mostly formed of dense granite.

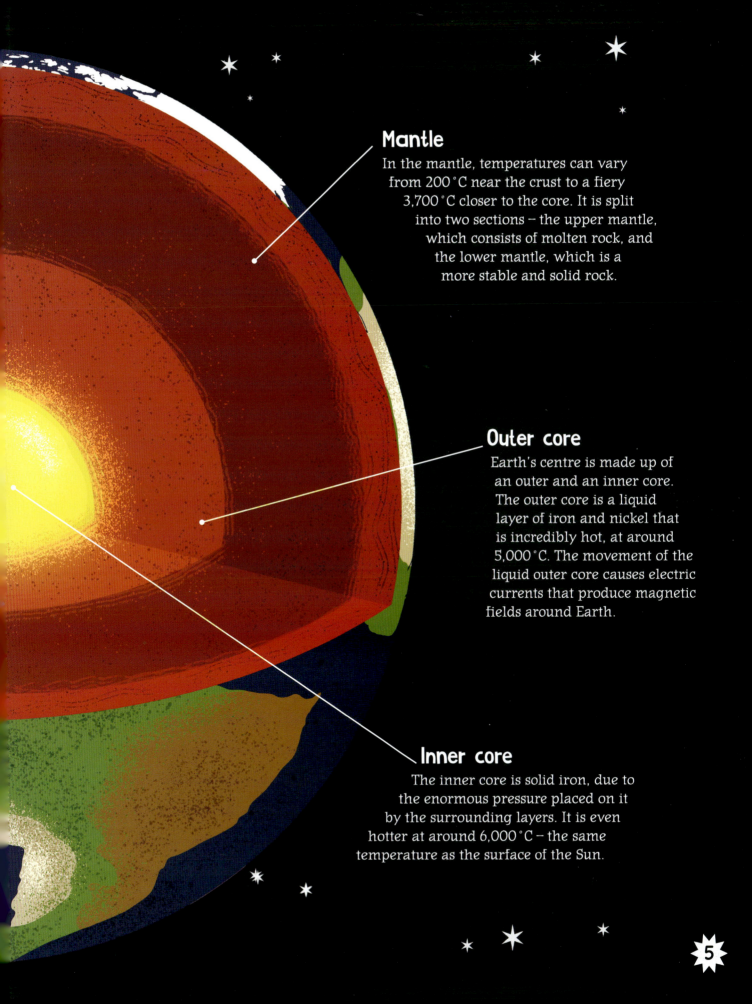

## Mantle

In the mantle, temperatures can vary from 200 °C near the crust to a fiery 3,700 °C closer to the core. It is split into two sections – the upper mantle, which consists of molten rock, and the lower mantle, which is a more stable and solid rock.

## Outer core

Earth's centre is made up of an outer and an inner core. The outer core is a liquid layer of iron and nickel that is incredibly hot, at around 5,000 °C. The movement of the liquid outer core causes electric currents that produce magnetic fields around Earth.

## Inner core

The inner core is solid iron, due to the enormous pressure placed on it by the surrounding layers. It is even hotter at around 6,000 °C – the same temperature as the surface of the Sun.

# TECTONIC PLATES

Earth's crust is split into large, rocky pieces, called tectonic plates. These fit together like a giant jigsaw puzzle. Where the plates meet, landscapes are constantly changing.

## Continental drift

Tectonic plates are always moving, very slowly, powered by heat currents in the Earth's molten mantle. As the plates shift, so do the continents on them. Over millions of years, Earth's land formations have kept changing, from the supercontinent Pangaea which formed about 270 million years ago (see below), to the ones we see today.

Europe
Asia
North America
PANGAEA
South America
Africa
India
Australia
Antarctica

## Moving together

The areas where two plates move towards each other are called convergent boundaries. Sometimes the plates at these boundaries push against each other, raising the landscape above to form mountains. Along other convergent boundaries, one plate may move under the other, forming deep ocean trenches.

## Moving apart

Two tectonic plates moving apart from each other share a divergent boundary. This movement leaves a gap, called a rift. Magma from the mantle keeps pushing up through the gap and solidifying. Africa's Great Rift Valley is a rare example of a divergent boundary that runs across land. Here, magma rises to the surface to form hot lava lakes.

Lava lake

## Sliding past

Sliding boundaries are found where two plates move alongside each other in opposite directions. This movement can cause the plates to catch on each other and create powerful earthquakes deep in the Earth's crust. Sometimes these earthquakes can destroy roads, buildings and whole areas of a city.

# ALWAYS CHANGING

Earth's crust is mainly made up of three different types of rock: igneous, metamorphic and sedimentary. All three form part of the rock cycle. This is a never-ending process by which rock is moved, broken down and changed.

Sediment is carried to lakes and oceans by rivers, streams and wind. Here, it settles and forms layers that are gradually pushed further underground.

Time and pressure can lead to sediment being compressed into **sedimentary** rock.

## Wearing away

Earth's surface is exposed to heat, cold, water and wind, which can gradually break rock down into tiny particles, or sediment. This process is called erosion.

When lava or magma cools down, it forms **igneous** rock.

## Metamorphic

When the heat and pressure reach a certain level, metamorphic rock forms and is gradually shifted to the surface.

The movement of tectonic plates can shift rocks into areas of extreme heat and pressure, such as convergent plate boundaries.

tectonic plate movement

# UNDER OUR FEET

In many places, the rock of Earth's crust is covered by soil. This material nourishes and anchors plants, provides a habitat for millions of animals, and even absorbs, filters and stores water.

## What is soil?

Soil is a mixture of living and dead organic materials, as well as minerals, air and water. Plants sprout and grow in soil, providing food for living things, and many insects, fungi and microorganisms start life here.

## Horizons

Soil builds up in layers, or horizons, and together these can be up to 50 m deep. As more soil gets added on the surface through processes such as decay and erosion (see pages 8–9), older layers are pushed further down.

Humus is made of decomposed plants and organisms.

**Topsoil** is a mixture of decayed matter, minerals and rock particles, as well as millions of organisms, from bacteria to bugs.

Organic matter

Decayed matter

Minerals

Fungi

Bacteria

# Some different types of rock found in the subsoil:

Pyrite

Turquoise

Howlite

Beryl

Sodalite

Schorl

Hematite

Cassiterite

**Subsoil** is firmer than topsoil and holds larger mineral and rock fragments.

Groundwater

Water level

## Groundwater

Water gradually trickles down through the soil. As it passes through air holes (pores) the water is filtered. This groundwater can saturate the ground above bedrock, forming aquifers. Many people dig wells to access aquifers for their drinking water.

**Regolith** is difficult to dig through, as it is the horizon where large pieces of rock settle.

**Bedrock** is a solid layer of rock that sits under all the soil horizons.

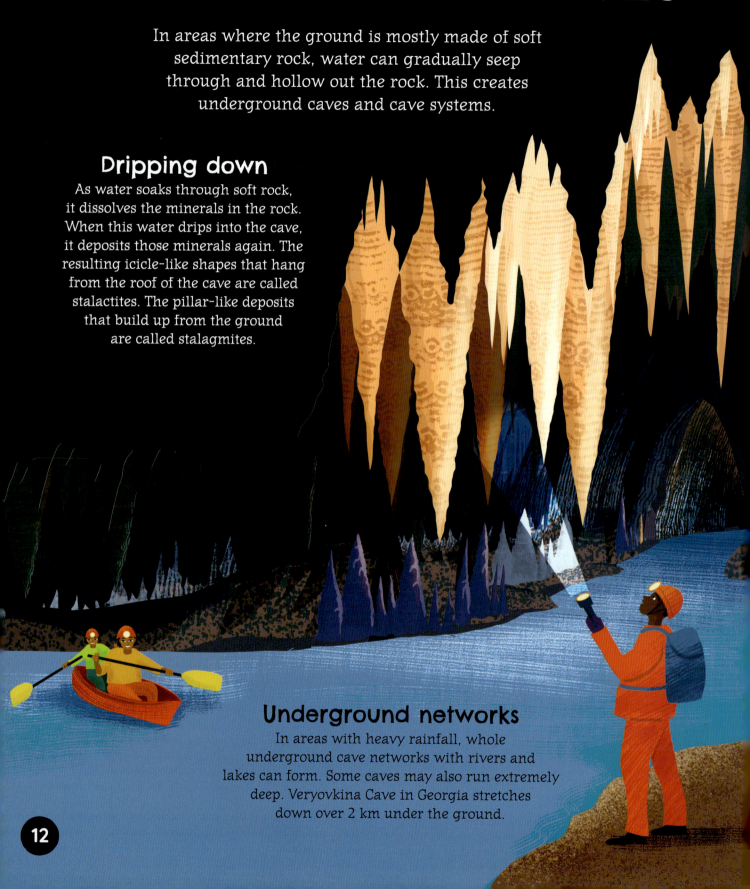

# UNDERGROUND CAVES

In areas where the ground is mostly made of soft sedimentary rock, water can gradually seep through and hollow out the rock. This creates underground caves and cave systems.

## Dripping down

As water soaks through soft rock, it dissolves the minerals in the rock. When this water drips into the cave, it deposits those minerals again. The resulting icicle-like shapes that hang from the roof of the cave are called stalactites. The pillar-like deposits that build up from the ground are called stalagmites.

## Underground networks

In areas with heavy rainfall, whole underground cave networks with rivers and lakes can form. Some caves may also run extremely deep. Veryovkina Cave in Georgia stretches down over 2 km under the ground.

# Lava tubes

In volcanic areas, a unique type of cave forms when lava forces its way through the earth. As the ground cools and hardens and the lava drains away, hollowed-out areas are left behind.

**1** Lava flow gradually forms a crust as the edges are cooled by the surrounding air.

**2** The crust encloses the still-hot lava as it continues to hollow out the ground.

**3** Lava retreats, leaving behind tube-shaped caves.

# Unique home

Lava tubes provide habitats for many microbes, as well as rare species of insect and spiders such as the eyeless Kaua'i cave wolf spider. Scientists study lava tubes to find out more about life in these extreme environments.

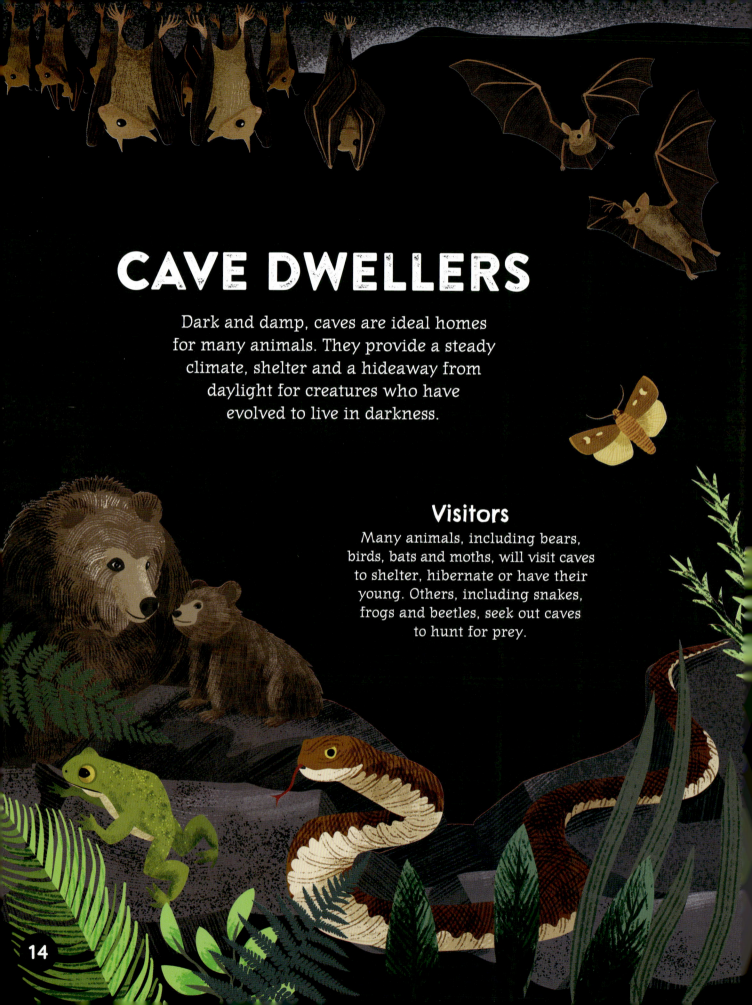

# CAVE DWELLERS

Dark and damp, caves are ideal homes
for many animals. They provide a steady
climate, shelter and a hideaway from
daylight for creatures who have
evolved to live in darkness.

## Visitors

Many animals, including bears,
birds, bats and moths, will visit caves
to shelter, hibernate or have their
young. Others, including snakes,
frogs and beetles, seek out caves
to hunt for prey.

## Cave slime

Some caves are covered in a slimy material that hangs down in long, dripping strings. This slime is home to bacteria that can survive the most extreme environments by creating this protective mucus to live in.

## At home in the dark

Animals that live in the constant darkness of caves are called troglobites. They have adapted to a life in darkness and could not survive outside of their caves. Often, they have sharp senses of hearing, touch and smell, but are blind or eyeless. Many troglobites are also white, because their bodies don't need any protection from the Sun.

# BURROWS

Underground spaces, dug by animals, are called burrows or dens. Different species seek out burrows to survive harsh temperatures or drought, to escape predators or to catch prey.

## In the desert

Deserts are hot by day and cool off rapidly by night. Animals such as kangaroo rats and desert tortoises dig burrows to shelter from the extreme temperatures. Spadefoot toads stay underground for weeks or months to protect their bodies from drying out until the rain arrives.

## Surviving winter

In areas where winters are particularly cold, animals like bears, insects and snakes go underground to shelter. While bears prefer to hibernate in dens close to the surface, some insects, such as wireworms, dig down up to 50 cm where the ground remains unfrozen.

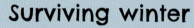

## Predator or prey

Some burrowers, such as funnel-web spiders, use burrows as a place to lie in wait and ambush their unlucky prey. Others, such as prairie dogs, create warrens or 'towns' – huge, complex underground tunnel systems – to avoid being captured by a predator.

# LIFE BELOW GROUND

Humans have built underground homes for thousands of years. Underground homes, houses carved into hillsides and cave dwellings offer shelter to people all around the world.

## House caves

In northern China, people carve *yaodong*, or 'house caves', out of the hillside to live in. Over 40 million people are believed to live in these unique homes. The design means that few extra building materials are required, and the temperatures remain cool in the summer and mild in the winter.

## Digging down

From above, Tunisia's town of Matmata looks like it is scattered with craters. These are actually round courtyards, dug deep into the ground and each surrounded by three or four cave homes. The homes are carved into sandstone, and have provided cool, safe homes for generations of families. They became world-famous when they were used as a filming location for some of the *Star Wars* movies.

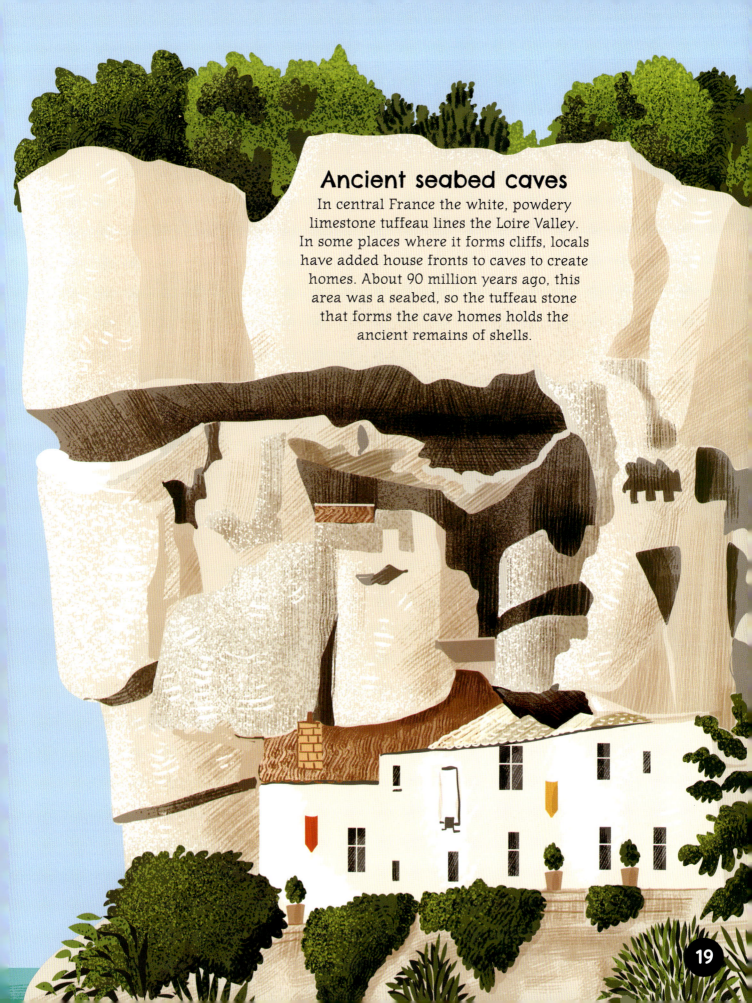

## Ancient seabed caves

In central France the white, powdery limestone tuffeau lines the Loire Valley. In some places where it forms cliffs, locals have added house fronts to caves to create homes. About 90 million years ago, this area was a seabed, so the tuffeau stone that forms the cave homes holds the ancient remains of shells.

# SAFE HIDEAWAYS

While underground spaces often serve as homes,
we also use them to shelter from danger. Bunkers,
tunnel systems and other underground shelters
can offer life-saving protection.

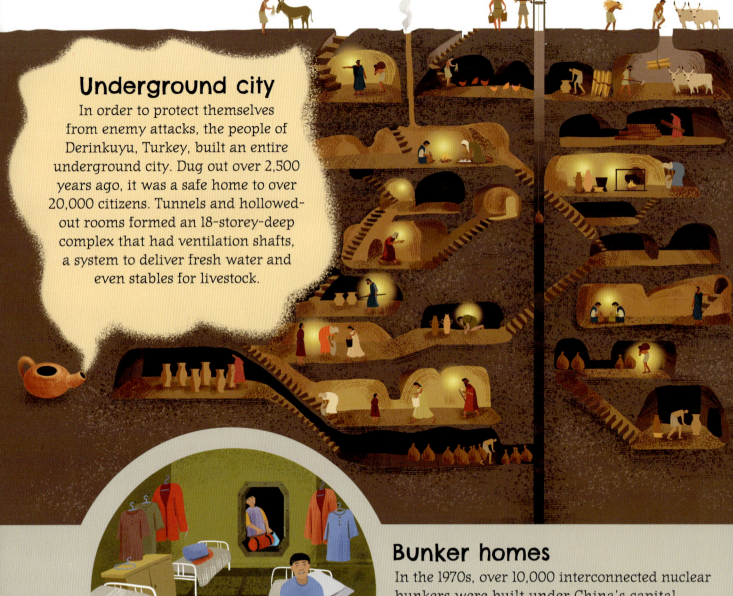

## Underground city

In order to protect themselves
from enemy attacks, the people of
Derinkuyu, Turkey, built an entire
underground city. Dug out over 2,500
years ago, it was a safe home to over
20,000 citizens. Tunnels and hollowed-
out rooms formed an 18-storey-deep
complex that had ventilation shafts,
a system to deliver fresh water and
even stables for livestock.

## Bunker homes

In the 1970s, over 10,000 interconnected nuclear
bunkers were built under China's capital,
Beijing. Today the bunkers offer affordable
housing to over a million people. Facilities
include shared bathrooms and kitchens,
as well as supermarkets and hairdressers.

# Mountain fortress

The Cheyenne Mountain Complex in Colorado, USA, is a high-security military base that was dug out of a granite mountain. Using over 680,000 kg of dynamite, a huge space was carved out that was so well shielded by its surrounding rock that it can withstand heavy attacks.

# HIDDEN NETWORKS

Beneath our feet lies a huge web of pipes, cables and tunnels supplying energy, water, sewage systems, communication and transport. From Internet access and running water to daily commutes, we all rely on these underground networks.

## Sanitation

As settlements have grown throughout history, so has the need to safely remove wastewater, in order to avoid outbreaks of dangerous diseases. Today, most homes are connected to large networks of underground tunnels, called sewage systems. Removing wastewater this way keeps homes safe and clean.

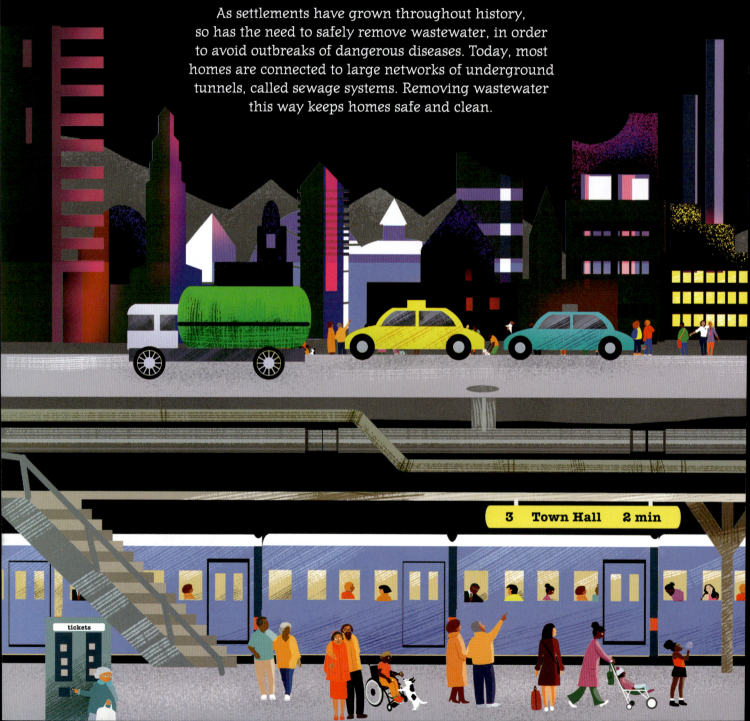

## Transport

In many cities, where different kinds of transport compete for space, and millions of people need to travel daily, whole networks of public transport are laid out underground. The most common of these is the underground railway. Here, trains speed through a system of tunnels, connecting different parts of a city and avoiding the busy streets.

## Beyond cities

Even outside dense, busy cities, going underground can be the fastest and safest way to travel. In mountainous areas, for example, tunnels protect traffic from extreme weather, rockfall and avalanches.

# UNDERGROUND RICHES

Buried deep underground are a wealth of precious resources, including minerals and fossil fuels. We extract, or mine, these materials using huge machines and modern technology.

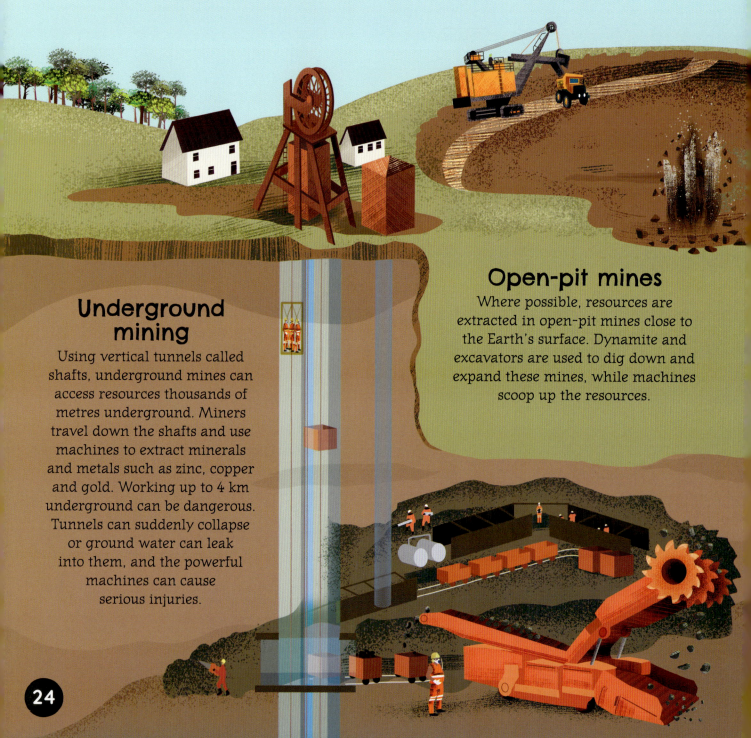

## Open-pit mines

Where possible, resources are extracted in open-pit mines close to the Earth's surface. Dynamite and excavators are used to dig down and expand these mines, while machines scoop up the resources.

## Underground mining

Using vertical tunnels called shafts, underground mines can access resources thousands of metres underground. Miners travel down the shafts and use machines to extract minerals and metals such as zinc, copper and gold. Working up to 4 km underground can be dangerous. Tunnels can suddenly collapse or ground water can leak into them, and the powerful machines can cause serious injuries.

# Drilling for energy

Oil and gas are important energy resources that are often found together, hundreds or thousands of metres underground. Both are extracted on land and offshore using wells that are drilled up to 5 km into the Earth's crust. Platforms in the ocean are engineered to withstand powerful storms while they access oil deep under the seabed.

# DIGGING UP THE PAST

When we are looking to uncover human history and clues about Earth's past, we often go underground. Here, remains, objects and sometimes even whole buildings lie preserved by layers of sediment, soil and rock.

## Prehistoric life

Palaeontologists dig to find fossils, which tell us about how life first evolved on Earth and what our planet looked like millions of years ago. Fossils are remains or traces of dead animals and plants that have been preserved over millions of years.

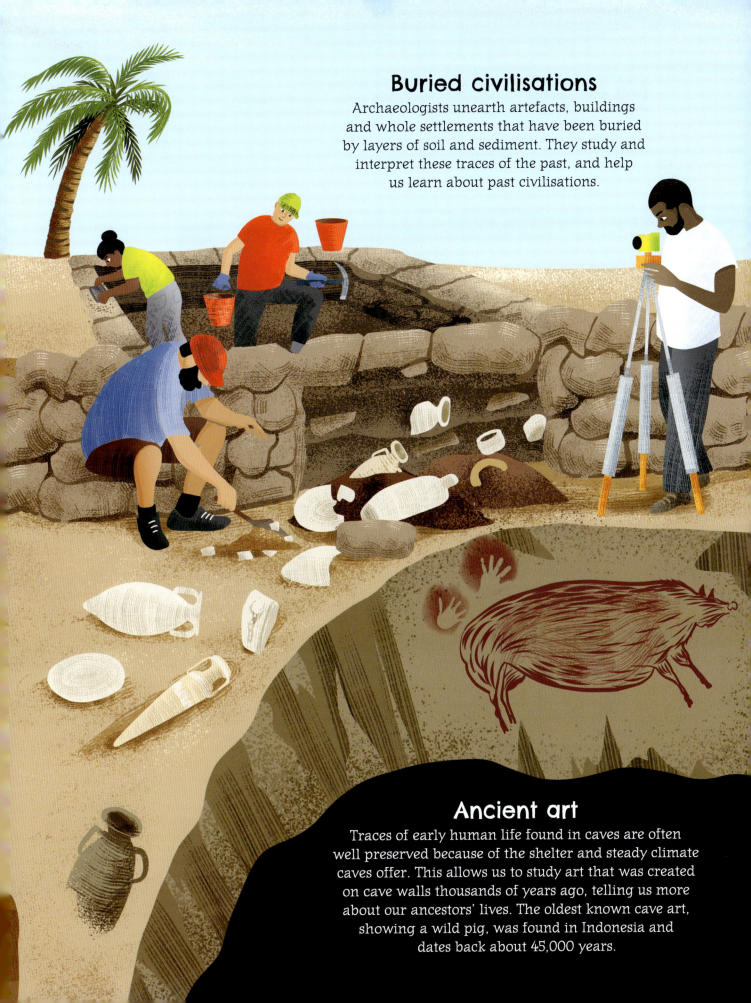

# Buried civilisations

Archaeologists unearth artefacts, buildings and whole settlements that have been buried by layers of soil and sediment. They study and interpret these traces of the past, and help us learn about past civilisations.

## Ancient art

Traces of early human life found in caves are often well preserved because of the shelter and steady climate caves offer. This allows us to study art that was created on cave walls thousands of years ago, telling us more about our ancestors' lives. The oldest known cave art, showing a wild pig, was found in Indonesia and dates back about 45,000 years.

# THE FUTURE

Climate change is causing Earth's weather patterns to shift and temperatures to gradually get warmer. Humans will need to adapt to these changes, and living underground may be one way of doing that.

## Escaping the heat

In Australia, the desert city of Coober Pedy is located in one of the hottest areas of the country. To escape the heat, most of the city has been built underground. Shops, hotels, schools and homes, known as 'dugouts', all offer modern comforts with steady cool temperatures, even during the hottest times of year.

## Creating space

With the world population steadily growing, cities and towns are starting to struggle for space. Finland's capital, Helsinki, has addressed this by creating a 'second city' underground. Here, facilities including shops, a swimming pool and a museum are all found below Earth's surface. This second city is also protected from Finland's harsh winters.

## Living on another planet

Scientists are investigating the possibility of humans setting up a base either on the Moon or on Mars. One of the many challenges will be keeping astronauts safe from radiation, meteorites and extreme temperatures. Lava tubes (see page 13) on the Moon and Mars could provide an ideal shelter from these threats.

# GLOSSARY

**ambush** to attack someone from a hiding place

**aquifer** a rocky area underground that holds large amounts of groundwater

**climate change** the gradual change of weather patterns

**deposit** to leave something behind or place it somewhere

**erosion** the process that gradually breaks down rock through heat, cold, wind and other environmental factor

**fungus (many fungi)** an organism that grows on plants or decayed matter; mushrooms are fungi

**groundwater** water that has filtered through the ground

**hibernation** to spend winter in a deep sleep-like statee

**igneous rock** when lava cools down, igneous rock forms

**lava** molten rock that flows from volcanoes

**magma** molten rock that is underground

**metamorphic rock** when rock is changed through heat or pressure, it becomes metamorphic rock

**meteorite** a piece of rock from space that reaches the surface of a planet or moon

**microbe** a microscopic organism

**microorganism** an organism such as a bacterium or virus that can only be seen with a microscope

**mineral** a hard, inorganic material that can be dug out of the ground

**nuclear reaction** chemical reaction that releases huge amounts of energy in the form of heat and radiation

**radiation** energy that can travel through space, such as light, radio waves, heat and X-rays

**rock cycle** the processes through which metamorphic, sedimentary and igneous rocks keep changing over time

**sediment** tiny solid particles

**saturated** when something has absorbed as much water as it can hold

**sedimentary rock** when sediment settles at the bottom of a lake or ocean and is compressed, it forms sedimentary rock

# DIG DEEPER

## Books

Aulenbach, Nancy Holler; Barton, Hazel and Delano, Marfé Ferguson: *Exploring Caves: Journeys into the Earth*; National Geographic Books, 2001

Martin, Claudia: *Geology Rocks – The Rock Cycle*; Wayland, 2023

Marshall, Geoff and Pipe, Vicki: *The London Underground: 50 Things to See and Do*; September Publishing, 2020

## Websites

www.caveslime.org/kids/cavejourney/index.html
Find out all about cave creatures and cave slime on this website, written by cave slime scientists!

www.myhelsinki.fi/en/see-and-do/underground-helsinki
Discover all the amazing underground facilities of Finland's capital city, Helsinki.

www.youtube.com/watch?v=NGtzSd3wFY4

This BBC Earth clip introduces some eyeless troglobites and explores how well they are adapted to life underground.

# INDEX

ambush 17
aquifer 11
archaeologists 27
artefacts 27

bacteria (one bacterium)
    10, 15
basalt 4
bats 14
bears 14, 16
beetles 14
bedrock 11
Beijing (China) 20
birds 14
bunkers 20
burrows 16–17

cave art 27
cave homes 18–19
caves 12–15, 18–19, 27
cave slime 15
cave systems 12
Cheyenne Mountain
    Complex 21
climate change 28
continental drift 6
Coober Pedy (Australia) 28
core (layer of Earth) 4–5
crust (layer of Earth) 4–8,
    10, 25

Derinkuyu (Turkey) 20
desert 16, 28
    tortoises 16
dugouts 28

earthquakes 7
erosion 8–10
extraterrestrial 29

fossil fuels 24–25
fossils 26

frogs 14
fungi (one fungus) 10

granite 4, 21
groundwater 11

Helsinki (Finland) 28
hibernate 14, 16
humus 10

igneous rock 8, 9
insects 16

kangaroo rats 16

lava 7, 9, 13, 29
lava lakes 7
lava tubes 13, 29

magma 4, 7, 9
magnetic fields 5
mantle (layer of Earth) 5–7
Mars 29
Matmata (Tunisia) 18
metal 4, 24
metamorphic rock 8–9
military 21
minerals 10–12, 24
mines 24
Moon 29
moths 14

ocean 4, 6, 8–9, 25
oil platforms 25

palaeontologists 26
Pangaea 6
prairie dogs 17
predator 14, 16–17
prey 14, 16–17
public transport 22–23

regolith 11
resources (natural) 24–25
rock cycle 8–9

sandstone 18
sediment 8–9, 26–27
sedimentary rock 8–9, 12
sewage systems 22'
snakes 14, 16
soil 10–11, 26
spadefoot toads 16
spiders 14
    Kaua'I cave wolf 13
    funnel web 17
stalactites 12
stalagmites 12
subsoil 11
Sun 5, 15

tectonic plate boundaries
    6–7
    convergent boundaries
    6, 9
    divergent boundaries 7
    sliding boundaries 7
tectonic plates 6–7, 9
topsoil 10
trenches (ocean) 6
troglobites 15
tuffeau stone 19
tunnels 17, 20, 22–23, 24

volcanoes 4, 9, 13

warrens 17
wells (oil) 25
wells (water) 10–11
winter 16, 18, 28
wireworms 16